Advance |
Church, Creation, an.

"Written from an Episcopal perspective, this curriculum helps facilitators guide a journey for Christian adult learners who seek to understand their faith in relationship to climate change. Heavy on theological foundations, the curriculum also provides concrete examples of how Christians are putting faith in action."

—Shantha Ready Alonso, Executive Director
of Creation Justice Ministries

"This timely, essential, and accessible curriculum will enable churches to begin theologically reflective, practically oriented, necessary conversations for our common future."

—Nurya Love Parish, founder of Plainsong
Farm and author of *Resurrection Matters*

"Ragan and Emily Sutterfield have put together an immensely helpful curriculum to help our congregations reflect on who we are and where we live in regards to the multitude of environmental challenges we face, including the changing climate. This book moves us into being a part of the solution and helps us become bearers of hope to this world."

—Bingham Powell, Rector of St. Mary's
Episcopal Church in Eugene, Oregon

"This curriculum couldn't be more urgently needed. Accessible and adaptable, sobering and hopeful, *Church, Creation, and the Common Good* offers scripturally sound, liturgically rooted ways of responding to the profound challenges of climate change, now and in the future."

—Debra Dean Murphy, associate professor of Religious
Studies at West Virginia Wesleyan College and
serves on the board of The Ekklesia Project

CHURCH, CREATION,

and the

COMMON GOOD

Guidance in an Age of Climate Crisis

Ragan Sutterfield
Emily Sutterfield

CHURCH
PUBLISHING
INCORPORATED

Church Publishing Incorporated
Editorial Offices
19 East 34th Street
New York, NY 10016

Cover design by: Jennifer Kopec, 2 Pug Design
Typeset by: PerfecType, Nashville, TN
Printed in the United States of America

A record of this book is available from the Library of Congress.

ISBN: 978-1-64065-111-1 (pbk.)
ISBN: 978-1-64065-112-8 (ebook)

CONTENTS

PREFACE

As we were finishing these session plans, record-breaking floods were affecting a large swath of the central United States. Suddenly, poor drainage systems were at their capacity and streets all around where we work and play were flowing with torrents of water. And yet, unlike other hot topics of the day such as racism, gun control, and immigration, we saw little to no discussion of the climate crisis in our churches. "The weather sure is strange," many people would say around the coffee hour table, but no one would then link that statement to how we inhabit the world.

We may feel that weather is the kind of thing about which we have no say or control, and so it seems to occupy a different place in our politics and practice than issues like racism. But the reality is that weather, though we cannot control it directly, is very much affected by the systems we embrace and the ways in which we live. Like racism, we are now reaping some of what our ancestors created and, just by accepting the status quo, we are still perpetuating the underlying systems that enforce it.

We need to talk about this reality. We need to name it and explore it and address it. And we need to start this work in our churches.

Why the Church? Because the Church is a place where we are concerned with the questions of human flourishing and right living within the context of a loving relationship with God. We are not beholden to election cycles or the economics of the market (at least we shouldn't be). We are concerned with the call of God and our faithful response, a response that might put us at odds with the systems of this world.

The world needs the Church to explore this critical crisis of our time, but for us to do so, we need to first talk with one another and discern what God is calling us to in our particular places. Only then can we offer life-giving possibilities to a world that is literally drowning in denial.

To begin this work we need to know what we are getting into. Here are some things to ponder before getting started.

Climate change is a complex and worrying issue.

Climate change is widely regarded as the most critical issue of our age, affecting global conflicts, poverty, economies, food supplies, and more. We find ourselves entangled in a situation we did not create and are scrambling to correct, though that correction will require significant changes to our most basic ways of life in modern, industrial countries. At the same time, climate disasters are already occurring. Whether it is rising sea levels threatening coastal communities or forest fires raging in the water-hungry West, our situation is one of increasingly unpredictable weather. Many people are deeply concerned about this reality, and therapists have begun to report increased visits from patients with environmentally induced anxieties. *Churches have a tremendous opportunity to show the love and peace of Christ in this age of climate anxiety.*

Creative and inspiring steps can be taken by churches.

The Church could be a place where skills for resilience and flourishing through the climate crisis are cultivated and disseminated.

Workshops on gardening, canning, and water collection would bring together community members. Churches could set up co-op structures to share space, time, and resources in more sustainable ways. Churches could be places that advocate and demonstrate steps to transition away from a lifestyle dependent on factors that contribute to climate change and into an alternative lifestyle of restoration. We invite you to help your group seek some of their own creative solutions together throughout this class. *Instead of fear and helplessness, we (as the Church) could offer hope and empowerment.*

We must stay informed and be prepared.

We highly recommend that facilitators and group members spend time researching some of these issues around climate change. Please find suggested readings and videos in Appendix E. Because climate change is constantly in flux and manifests differently in various locations, we suggest that for each section you come up with your own vision and findings before leading the class. It is best to have local examples of your own to share in connection with each section. *In this way, we can practice a version of the advice of the famous theologian Karl Barth to "take your Bible and take your newspaper, and read both. But interpret newspapers from your Bible."*[1]

Here's how this curriculum takes a different approach.

This curriculum sets out to address these challenges by taking on climate change from a different direction than it is often approached in church. First, we assume climate change as a reality that is here and will have catastrophic effects no matter what people do at this

---

1. From "Barth in Retirement," *Time Magazine*, Friday, May 31, 1963. http://content.time.com/time/magazine/article/0,9171,896838,00.html (accessed March 12, 2018).

point. This is important because it changes how we respond. Unlike many programs that have tried to prevent climate change, this program asks how do we properly live as Church in the midst of the climate crisis and work to be resilient communities in our particular places? Second, this curriculum works to engage a broad base within the Church by using the questions the climate crisis raises as a way to think about who we are as Church in this time and place. Our hope is that climate skeptics as well as enthusiastic "green-team" members will both fully engage this study and unify around the practices we call for rather than around a common worldview. *We do hope that worldview change will come, but we believe that practices are more fundamental than ideas and that ideas will change in response to practices.*

INTRODUCTION

This program resource started with a visit to Florida. Along the south-west coast, we visited a small Episcopal church involved in a number of ministries locally and abroad. They were proud of their fundraisers for struggling communities in Haiti that were suffering from the results of earthquakes and other disasters, and for their work with local people experiencing homelessness. Yet this church had little awareness or connection to the climate crisis that was literally rising all around them.

Current climate models show the coast of southwest Florida disappearing over the coming centuries through the slow but ever accelerating rise of the oceans. Already, local funding goes into sending truckloads of sand to the beaches that are disappearing more and more each year. Yet life is continuing as usual.

We came to this particular part of Florida hoping to see innovative models of how churches are dealing with the climate crisis, yet we found that most are simply following the pattern of the rest of us—the seas rise, but no one is talking about it.

According to models of the impact climate change will have over the next century, Florida is predicted to face some of the most profound challenges of all. Landscapes will change drastically. Life cannot continue as it has over the past two hundred years. Change is inevitable for these communities.

Already, the weather and landscape are transforming. Hurricanes have become more severe and unseasonable. As massive sheets of ice melt into the ocean far away, sea levels are noticeably rising in spots along the coast of Florida. But when we tried to discuss these issues by phone and in person with different church groups in the area, we were often told that it is a difficult subject to address and nothing more came of it.

So we started to ask some questions, not only for churches in Florida but for churches everywhere. How might we serve God and our neighbor in a time of climate crisis? Are we in denial or simply unaware of the severity of the crisis? Did churches believe the question was too political and therefore wanted to avoid it altogether? Or was climate change simply too overwhelming to address? Perhaps the answer was a mixture of all of these concerns and more.

We started to wonder if this was just too tough an issue for churches to tackle. Then we stepped back and tried to imagine answers from a different angle. We started to look for creative examples of churches taking hopeful steps with regard to climate change, even if the issues weren't being directly discussed and addressed.

We found a Methodist Church in southwest Florida that offered some answers in small, yet deep ways for their community. They were doing it through relationship. Relationship with the different groups of people living in their neighborhood—long-term residents as well as migrant laborers. Relationship with their environment, like the watershed and soil. Not only did they worship and pray together, they also offered hurricane disaster relief to victims of storms. They created a permaculture farm on the empty lots by the church and generously shared the produce. They strived to know and love their land and people well. This church's leader seemed to be fearless in the face of difficult questions and pushed his congregation to be fearless as well.

From there, we visited a faith-based training center offering support to young farmers and agricultural development workers around the world. They experiment with appropriate solutions to the changing landscapes of our time. We observed some solutions such as seed-banks, water conservation tools, and new ways to grow food that require little money and infrastructure. We started to envision churches learning from such places—learning to be places of boldness and hope in the face of climate crisis.

Our visit to Florida was not as we imagined it would be. We were hoping to learn from churches that are directly dealing with the realities of climate change today. We were surprised that so little was being discussed and addressed.

But these later visits to the Methodist church and training facility helped us realize a few things:

- Creative and proactive steps that give folks hope are occurring.
- Deep relationship with local place and people can be nurtured.
- Churches cannot be silent any longer but need to be sensitive when addressing the issue of climate change.

After our trip to Florida, we spent time prayerfully outlining a way to address some of these issues. We combined various stories, reflections, prayers, and discussion topics to guide the process. What follows is a resource to help local congregations start looking at their church's role in a time of climate crisis.

This Study

What follows is a six-week course that seeks to engage the Church in the challenges climate change poses to our age. This class is broken into three main sections: *Ecclesia, Ecology,* and *Economy.* There will be two sessions connected to each section.

In the first section, *Ecclesia*, we focus on the resources and traditions of the Church. We begin not by looking at what climate change is but by looking at what the Church is. Then we move from that understanding to an exploration of how the Church should engage with climate change.

In the next section, *Ecology*, we start to explore the Church's relationship with home and place: where we live, who and what we live among, and so forth. Through a variety of exercises, we hope to reshape our view of the Church's connection to the wider neighborhood and community in the face of climate change.

In the last section, *Economy*, we examine our personal and collective responsibilities as we care for our households and use the goods of our places in ways that enable us to care for the common good of all, now and in the future.

In each section, we will invite you to identify and work from the assets of your community (rather than the deficits) with a goal toward flourishing for all. Together we can imagine how the Church can provide bold and new ways to move forward, not only in addressing climate change but other modern issues as well. Through an exploration of *Ecclesia*, *Ecology*, and *Economy*, it is our hope that churches can draw on their traditions and practices to become the *Communities for the Common Good* that the world needs now.

Facilitators and Participants

This publication serves as both a resource for facilitators and a participant's book. Your group may wish to share the leadership of facilitation, choosing a different leader each week; or you may wish to assign or rotate different leadership roles: worship leader, discussion facilitator, and scribe. There is space provided for individual journaling or notes the facilitator wishes to make.

It is our hope to make this an accessible resource and study guide for large groups and small, with the goal of having a plan of action at its conclusion. All prayers and scriptures used are contained within the session plans, and the materials listed that will be needed are ones that are easily gathered in advance.

The Session Plans

This curriculum is deeply Episcopal in that it relies and draws on the prayers and liturgies of the *Book of Common Prayer*. Yet our hope is that Christ-followers of all traditions will be able to adapt this material to their own patterns of life and worship. Feel free to change parts of the sessions to fit your particular context.

There is a basic format for facilitating this curriculum through six consistent sessions that build upon each other. Included are ways to grow and expand the sessions through documentaries, connections with local experts, and ideas for hands-on projects. Modify and use these suggestions as you see fit for your particular group.

The basic framework breaks down each session into one-hour segments. Each session could definitely last longer through deeper discussions. We have strived to give congregations starting points, but our hope is that this will foster conversation and action steps beyond the group meetings.

Lastly, we suggest offering this as a Sunday morning option for your church group. This is how it was piloted. This time slot seems to draw in a variety of participants that might not otherwise have joined. Yet an evening course or weekend option could be a great gift to your church as well.

Our hope is that, as churches use this curriculum, we can learn from one another. What works? What could grow? What particular locations could use the curriculum in more direct ways (for example, setting up shelters for storm victims)? What creative steps do churches take that can offer others hope and direction? The Church needs a network to start addressing this difficult challenge of climate change together.

SESSION 1

Ecclesia, Part 1

Objectives

- To gain a clear perspective on what the Church should be
- To reflect on the Church as a Truth-Telling Community
- To explore the Church as an Agent of God's Work
- To deepen our understanding of the Church as a Vision of the Future

Materials

- ❏ Flip chart
- ❏ Markers
- ❏ Pens
- ❏ Images and key words, each cut out separately in advance from magazines and newspapers that remind you of possible ways to define the Church. (You may choose to have magazines, newspapers, and scissors available for participants to find their own as an extended activity.)

1

❏ Blank sheets of paper
❏ One copy of *Church, Creation, and the Common Good* for each participant

Reminders for the Facilitator

- Organize and set up the room with all materials ahead of time.
- Pray for all the participants before each session.
- Keep the conversation flowing, making room for all to share.
- Be open to listening more than sharing.
- Let the process unfold organically for each participant.

Welcome and Opening Prayer   (5 minutes)

Welcome to the first session of the class *Church, Creation, and the Common Good*. Make sure everyone has a seat where they can be seen and heard. Let them know that this will be a time of prayerful discernment together. You are there as a facilitator who is open to learn and grow with them.

During this first class, if there is adequate time, give each participant a chance to introduce themselves. Let them know who you are as well. If it is appropriate, share a bit about why you felt called to lead this class and invite everyone to share why they are interested in the topic.

Explain that during each session, we will open with a time of prayer. Read aloud the following prayer or allow a volunteer to read it aloud for the group.

> Keep, O Lord, your household the Church in your steadfast faith and love, that through your grace we may proclaim your truth with boldness, and minister your justice with compassion; for the sake of our Savior Jesus Christ,

who lives and reigns with you and the Holy Spirit, one God, now and forever. *Amen.*[2]

Session Overview   (15 minutes)

Share:

In our first two sessions, we will be exploring what it means to be the Church. We are talking about Church in capital letters—not just about the one particular church we may be part of (though our particular church is a local representation of the Church at large). We sometimes refer to the Christian Church as *Ecclesia*.

Questions to Ponder:

- Thinking back to the prayer we just read, we are reminded that we are called to be "the Church" in faith and love. What does that mean?
- What is "the Church"?
- How do we define "the Church"?

After a few moments of silence, scatter the cut-out images and words on the floor in the middle of your circle.

- Choose a word or image that speaks to you when thinking of how you define "the Church."
- Have blank paper as well. If you choose, you can draw your own image or write in your own word as well.

Go around the group and have everyone share their images or words with the group. Each participant can briefly explain why they chose their particular word or image. No one needs to share if they are not comfortable.

As specific thoughts are shared, write them on a flip chart.

---

2. "Collect for Proper 6," *Book of Common Prayer*, 230.

Focus for the Day   (5 minutes)

Thank the group for sharing their thoughts. Explain in your own words that we all have many different ways of understanding the Church and it is indeed many things. The Church is a community, a people, an Agent of God's mission in the world. The Church can mean different things to different people at different seasons of their lives. All of this is important to be aware of and to respect.

The Church can also be very powerful. Therefore, we must continually reflect on what it *should* be through prayer and humility, and through study and conversation. How can we go deeper together to understand the Church?

To explore the meaning of "Church" more deeply, let us start by going to prayer and scripture. Prayers help us define our theology. Scripture serves as the authoritative guide for our lives. *Lex orandi, lex credendi:* It is prayer that leads to belief and it is liturgy that leads to theology.

We will use these two sources of prayer and scripture to help us better understand what the Church is supposed to be.

Break into pairs or smaller groups. Each team can have a different prayer and scripture to explore together. The facilitator should float between groups to help them stay on track in their conversations. (See Appendix A, pages 47–50.)

Group Reflection   (20 minutes)

Give the small groups plenty of time to discuss their prayers and scriptures. Encourage them to take notes and to be ready to share their key findings with the larger group.

Optional: Each group can come up with one image and word to define the Church together. Based on their particular scriptures or prayers, they can select from the leftover images and words of the first activity.

After time for reflection, gather everyone back together. Give each group time to briefly share their prayers and scriptures, summarizing what they discovered in their exploration of the prayers and scriptures.

Optional: If they choose a word and image, they can share and post these on blank chart paper. Each group can add to the same page, creating one large poster together.

After everyone has had a chance to share, take time to sum up the key points.

Key Points and Next Steps   (10 minutes)

From our readings and discussion, we have hopefully deepened our understanding of what the Church is about. Sometimes it is good to clear our perspectives and focus on key points.

Based on our readings, three important points stand out (write each heading on a flip chart sheet to use in later sessions):

1. *Truth-Telling Community*
   God has called the Church to be a community that tells the Truth to each other and to the world. Throughout the week, think of what that means to be a Truth-Telling Community.

2. *Agents of God's Work*
   God has called the Church to be an Agent of God's Work for renewing the world and restoring the common good. Throughout the week, think of what it means to be Agents of God's work.

3. *Vision of Hope for the Future*
   God has called the Church to be a community that lives in the now but is guided by what God is working for in the future. Throughout the week, think of what it means to be a Vision of Hope for the Future.

In preparation for the next session:

- Look around for examples of people or groups that are living into our call to be the Church.
- Where in our community do you see people living into Truth?
- Where in the world do you see groups living as Agents of God's work?
- Where do you see communities living into hopeful visions of how God's Kingdom should be?

These may be examples within or outside of the Church. Come back ready to share what you find; bring images if you choose.

Closing Prayer   (5 minutes)

Close with *Prayers of the People, Form I* found in Appendix B on page 51. Encourage participants to add in their own petitions throughout the prayer. Volunteers can read different sections if you'd like.

Ecclesia, Part 2

Objectives

- To understand practical ways the Church can be a Truth-telling community, an Agent for God's work, and a Vision of the Future
- To reflect on challenges the Church needs to address and to focus more deeply on the issue of climate change
- To deepen our understanding of how the Church can work for the common good in the face of climate change

Materials

- ❏ Flip chart
- ❏ Markers
- ❏ Pens
- ❏ Paper
- ❏ Chart paper with "3 Key Factors of Church" written on it: 1. Truth-Telling Community; 2. Agent of God's Work; 3. Vision of Hope for the Future

❏ One copy of *Church, Creation, and the Common Good* for each participant who did not receive one in the first session

❏ *Optional:* Screen, computer, LCD player, or other connection to show videos

Reminders for the Facilitator

- Organize and set up the room and materials ahead of time.
- Pray for all the participants before each session.
- Keep the conversation flowing, making room for all to share.
- Be open to listening more than sharing.
- Let the process unfold organically for each participant.

Welcome and Opening Prayer   (5 minutes)

Welcome the group back to the class. Give everyone time to find a seat. If there is anyone who is new, invite them to introduce themselves.

Give a brief overview of the last session in which we started to explore our role as Ecclesia, the Church. In this session, we are going to go deeper into that understanding of being the Church by looking at specific, real-life examples together.

Begin with an opening prayer. Read this aloud or ask for a volunteer to share it:

> Generous Giver,
> you pour forth your extravagant bounty without measure
> upon your whole creation.
> Teach us such generosity,
> that the fruits of our spirits
> and the works of our hands may build
> your commonwealth of blessing. *Amen.*[3]

---

3. *Daily Prayer for All Seasons* (New York: Church Publishing, 2014), 123.

Session Overview   (15 minutes)

Share:

In our last class, we explored what the Church is supposed to be. Refer to the chart that is posted at the front of the room. Review that we ended the class by focusing on three important aspects of the Church:

1. The Church as a Truth-Telling Community
2. The Church as an Agent for God's Work
3. The Church as a Vision of Hope for the Future

Invite participants to share any observations from the last week of real-life examples for the Church to learn from. Remind them that at the end of the last class you asked for them to look for signs of Truth-Telling Communities, Agents of God's Work, and Visions of Hope for the Future. Take time for all to share with the group; also add your own examples if there is time and if it is needed.

Optional: Some participants may have brought pictures, articles, or other artifacts to share. More time can be devoted to these findings if appropriate.

Thank everyone for sharing. Describe how we are going to continue to look at how the Church can live more fully into these practices to create *Communities for the Common Good*.

Questions to Ponder:

- When you look at the world today, what are the greatest challenges that we face—for people, the environment, all of creation?
- Where do we see suffering in our local and global communities that may seem overwhelming?

Give a few moments for participants to share some of the big challenges that came to mind for them. Let them briefly share key words or phrases at this time. *Note:* This is not yet the moment for deep discussion.

Focus for the Day   (5 minutes)

Our work as the Church is to be aware of our connections to these challenges and to be prayerfully responsive as well.

Today we are going to pull out one big challenge that may directly or indirectly affect many of the problems that we have shared. We are going to focus on the crisis of climate change. Encourage the group to think back to the list of challenges that they shared (and others as well). How many of those problems can be connected to climate change? Let them think on this but not share aloud.

After a time of reflection, give an example: Many people are without homes today due to major storms, flooding, fires, and other natural disasters. The increasing number and severity of these disasters are directly connected to climate change.

The problem of climate change is unique and complex. Most political, economic, and moral systems are unable to successfully deal with this issue. They tend to either argue about or ignore the problem altogether.

We hope to explore together how the Church can grapple with climate change in a practical and transformative way. We, as the Church, can be bold and hopeful together in the face of climate change.

Group Reflection   (20 minutes)

To start this process, we need to look at what climate change is and why it is so problematic.

You have a few options for leading this part of the session:

- You can show a short video (or a long video) to the entire class. (See Appendix E on page 60 for suggestions.) Then you can follow up by reading some specific facts about climate change. (See Appendix D on page 58.)

- Or you can skip the video and just read and discuss the facts in small groups or the large group together.

After the video (if you choose to show it), break the group into three smaller groups. Assign each group an aspect of the Church to focus on as well, referring to the chart that is posted. Give one group "Church as a Truth-Telling Community," one group "Church as an Agent for God's Work," and one group "Church as a Vision of Hope for the Future." Encourage each group to think through their particular focus of the Church in relation to climate change.

Post various questions for them to choose to start out with as a group on the flip chart:

- What concerns about the impacts of climate change do you have personally?
- Which impacts do you feel are greatest?
- Do you believe that climate change is a big problem?
- Why is climate change such a difficult issue to address?

Additional questions to share with the different groups:

- For the "Truth-Telling Community" group:
    — How do our fears affect our perception of climate change?
    — How does faith change our relationship with fear?
    — How does faith change our relationship with Truth?
    — When we think of being a Truth-Telling Community with regard to climate change, what thoughts come to mind?
- For the "Agent of God's Work" group:
    — If our call as Christians is to care for our neighbors, particularly those who are poor and vulnerable, how do we make sense of this call in an age of climate change?
    — How can we nurture for peace and justice for the poor and oppressed in the face of climate change?

- For the "Vision of Hope for the Future" group:
  — What are ways we can wake up as a Church to a new vision of hope and action?
  — What are the lifestyles and desires we may need to refuse to gratify?
  — How do we live into the world as it should be, respecting all of creation?

After the participants have had time to reflect, bring them all back together. Briefly share words or thoughts that popped up during this time.

Our reactions to climate change can be varied. Some of us may feel skepticism, fear, helplessness, and anger about this issue. Some may simply want to avoid it altogether. Climate change is definitely an overwhelming problem.

If there is time, go deeper into why climate change is so difficult to address. Then share the following ideas if they have not already come up:

- *It is a unique moral problem.* It is hard to assign clear blame of who started it and who needs to fix it.
- *It is a multigenerational problem.* It started long ago and will affect those more greatly in generations to come.
- *It is an entangled problem.* We are all connected to it by our daily lives and it is difficult to see how to untangle ourselves.
- *It is a confusing scientific problem.* There are complex and incomplete scientific explanations that lead to possibilities for confusion and disinformation.
- *It is unclear if it is a solvable problem.* There is no clear course of action to take; something must be done, but it may require major changes on many levels.

Key Points and Next Steps   (10 minutes)

Given the nature of this problem, how can the Church, as a community for the common good, offer hope and boldness?

Explain that the Church has a long tradition of living as a community now in a way that is oriented toward God's Truth and to a future of hope. This is why we say, "Thy Kingdom come, thy will be done."

This was particularly true for the Church in Rome when the apostle Paul wrote to them. They had a sense that God's reign was coming soon and that they should live into that reality rather than just going about their lives as normal.

If there is time, share this passage from Romans. Invite a volunteer to read portions of it as well.

> "Make sure that you don't get so absorbed and exhausted in taking care of all your day-by-day obligations that you lose track of the time and doze off, oblivious to God. The night is about over, dawn is about to break. Be up and awake to what God is doing! God is putting the finishing touches on the salvation work he began when we first believed. We can't afford to waste a minute, must not squander these precious daylight hours in frivolity and indulgence, in bickering and grabbing everything in sight. Get out of bed and get dressed! Don't loiter and linger, waiting until the very last minute. Dress yourselves in Christ, and be up and about!" —Romans 13.1–14 from *The Message*

In preparation for the next session:

During the next week, encourage the group to spend time prayerfully considering these verses in light of their discussions.

- How can the church take tangible steps that lead to healing and hope in the face of climate change?
- Look for ways that climate change is showing up in the world, particularly in places close to home.
- Bring in newspaper articles and stories to share with the group if they'd like.

Finally, for groups that are able to have a dedicated space or flip chart for the duration of the class, have a place for a chart of the major themes covered under the *Ecclesia* section of the course. Charts can grow and evolve in one space as folks add words, images, or drawings to each section. Let this be as simple or as elaborate as you see fit for the group. These will be helpful as we review and finish the course as well as spark interest and inform members of the congregation who are not participating in the course.

Closing Prayer   (5 minutes)

Read the following prayer, which is a free translation of the Lord's Prayer, or invite a participant to read it aloud.

> Our Loving Caretaker who is above all, holy is your name. May your reign arrive and all things live in harmony with you, here as in all places. Give us what we need for today, and release us from what we owe as we offer release to those who owe us. Keep us from the dangerous places and save us from evil. For yours is the authority, the power, and the beauty. *Amen.*

SESSION 3

Ecology, Part 1

Objectives

- To understand how *Ecclesia* (the Church) connects to *Ecology* (our home) through Incarnation
- To reflect on God's household and the household of creation in this time of climate change
- To deepen our understanding of our connections to creation and to others as the Church

Materials

- ❏ Flip chart
- ❏ Markers
- ❏ Pens
- ❏ Paper
- ❏ Chart paper with "3 Key Factors of Church" written on it: 1. Truth-Telling Community; 2. Agent of God's Work; 3. Vision of Hope for the Future

❑   Chart paper with "Ecclesia → Ecology" (written in bold print)
❑   One copy of *Church, Creation, and the Common Good* for
    each participant who did not receive one in a previous session

Reminders for the Facilitator

- Organize and set up the room and materials ahead of time.
- Pray for all the participants before each session.
- Keep the conversation flowing, making room for all to share.
- Be open to listening more than sharing.
- Let the process unfold organically for each participant.

Welcome and Opening Prayer   (5 minutes)

Welcome the group back to the class. Give everyone time to find a
seat. If there is anyone who is new to the class, let them introduce
themselves.

Give a brief overview of where we have journeyed thus far. During
the last two classes, we explored our role as *Ecclesia*, the Church. We
started to look at our connections to challenges in the world and how
to be the Church in response to them. We dug deeper into our roles,
specifically in response to the crisis of climate change.

In this session, we are going to start to connect *Ecclesia* (the
Church) to *Ecology* (our home), the place where we live. We will continue to keep in mind the issue of climate change as we make these
connections.

Read aloud the following prayer or ask for a volunteer to share it
with the group.

> Almighty and everlasting God, you made the universe
> with all its marvelous order, its atoms, worlds, and galax-
> ies, and the infinite complexity of living creatures: Grant
> that, as we prove the mysteries of your creation, we may

come to know you more truly, and more surely fulfill our role in your eternal purpose; in the name of Jesus Christ our Lord. *Amen.*[4]

Session Overview   (15 minutes)

Remind the class how we started to examine climate change from the perspective of the Church as a Truth-Telling Community, the Church as an Agent of God's Work and, the Church as a Vision of Hope for the Future.

Share:

Invite participants to share any findings they discovered over the week. Did they read new stories or find articles or thoughts to share with the group about climate change?

When we think of how overwhelming these issues may be with regard to the entire world, let us start to think from a more focused perspective of the particular places where we live. Let us go back to the roots of our Christian faith where Christ became flesh and blood in a particular place. He set up his home on the earth.

Write *eco = oikos* on the flip chart. *Eco* comes from the Greek word for home, which is *oikos*. This term was used by early naturalists to describe the web of relationships within creation; they said this web was like a great household. The study of this household is called ecology. Write *Ecology* on the chart.

Questions to Ponder:
- As we are Christ's body now incarnate on earth, how do we come to understand this household in which we exist?
- How do we come to understand our place?

---

4. "For Knowledge of God's Creation," *Book of Common Prayer*, 827.

- How do we make sense of the web in which we are all connected?

Explain that during this class we are going to dig deeper into our connections to this web of life, particularly in the ways it connects with our faith. We will first go to the Incarnation so we can better understand the Ecology of our particular place and time.

Group Reflection   (20 minutes)

Break into three smaller groups. Assign each group one of the following pieces of scripture and a few questions to discuss.

Group One
  Read John 1:1–18:

> In the beginning was the Word, and the Word was with God, and the Word was God. He was in the beginning with God. All things came into being through him, and without him not one thing came into being. What has come into being in him was life, and the life was the light of all people.
>
> The light shines in the darkness, and the darkness did not overcome it. There was a man sent from God, whose name was John. He came as a witness to testify to the light, so that all might believe through him. He himself was not the light, but he came to testify to the light. The true light, which enlightens everyone, was coming into the world. He was in the world, and the world came into being through him; yet the world did not know him. He came to what was his own, and his own people did not accept him. But to all who received him, who believed in his name, he

gave power to become children of God, who were born,
not of blood or of the will of the flesh or of the will of man,
but of God. And the Word became flesh and lived among
us, and we have seen his glory, the glory as of a father's
only son, full of grace and truth.

(John testified to him and cried out, "This was he
of whom I said, 'He who comes after me ranks ahead of
me because he was before me.'") From his fullness we
have all received, grace upon grace. The law indeed was
given through Moses; grace and truth came through Jesus
Christ. No one has ever seen God. It is God the only Son,
who is close to the Father's heart, who has made him
known.

Discuss what the Incarnation means:

- What does it mean for God's word to take on flesh in Jesus?
- As Christ's body now incarnate on earth, how do we come to understand the household and place where we exist?
- How do we make sense of the web by which we are all connected?

Group Two
Read Luke 22:14–20:

When the hour came, he took his place at the table, and
the apostles with him. He said to them, "I have eagerly
desired to eat this Passover with you before I suffer; for I
tell you, I will not eat it until it is fulfilled in the Kingdom
of God." Then he took a cup, and after giving thanks he
said, "Take this and divide it among yourselves; for I tell
you that from now on I will not drink of the fruit of the
vine until the Kingdom of God comes." Then he took a
loaf of bread, and when he had given thanks, he broke it
and gave it to them, saying, "This is my body, which is

given for you. Do this in remembrance of me." And he
did the same with the cup after supper, saying, "This
cup that is poured out for you is the new covenant in my
blood."

Discuss what the Incarnation means:

- What does it mean for the body of Christ to be incarnate in
  the Eucharist?
- As Christ's body now incarnate on earth, how do we come to
  understand the household and place where we exist?
- How do we make sense of the web by which we are all
  connected?

Group Three
Read Romans 12:3–8:

> For by the grace given to me I say to everyone among
> you not to think of yourself more highly than you ought
> to think, but to think with sober judgment, each accord-
> ing to the measure of faith that God has assigned. For
> as in one body we have many members, and not all the
> members have the same function, so we, who are many,
> are one body in Christ, and individually we are members
> one of another. We have gifts that differ according to the
> grace given to us: prophecy, in proportion to faith; minis-
> try, in ministering; the teacher, in teaching; the exhorter,
> in exhortation; the giver, in generosity; the leader, in dili-
> gence; the compassionate, in cheerfulness.

Discuss what the Incarnation means.

- What does it mean for the body of Christ to be incarnate in
  the Church?
- As Christ's body now incarnate on earth, how do we come to
  understand the household and place where we exist?

- How do we make sense of the web by which we are all connected?

After each group has time to discuss their thoughts with one another, bring the entire class back together. Encourage each group to summarize their scripture and the key points that surfaced from their conversations.

Ask them to think about what these three verses have in common. Explain that each scripture offers one of the three ways the New Testament discusses the body of Christ. Christ's Incarnation is about God's Word taking on flesh—in Jesus, in the Eucharist, and in the Church. John speaks of the incarnate body of Christ in Jesus, Luke talks about the body of Christ in the Eucharist, and Paul in Romans speaks about the Body of Christ as the Church.

Key Points and Next Steps   (10 minutes)

The three bodies of Christ help remind us that Jesus exists not as some abstract reality but as a person embedded in the reality of the creation.

By being embodied, Christ is connected in relationship with the whole of the creation. Christ ate food grown in dirt. Christ's body had all of the bacteria and fungi that make healthy human life possible. Christ was dependent upon clean water and air. Christ became part of the context of life that enables us to be human.

Through His presence in the bread and wine, we are all connected to soil, water, sun, yeast, and a host of other organisms that nurture growth.

As a Church that is the incarnation of Christ today, we are part of a neighborhood, part of a context, and part of an ecosystem.

In preparation for the next session:

Begin to think about the neighborhood, the place, the ecosystem where we live. What are we connected to?

Give each participant a different topic to focus on, or post all of these topics on the flip chart and encourage them to choose what they are most interested in. The purpose is to research their connections to their ecosystem more deeply. Links to organizations with data are listed in Appendix E.

- *What are the major trees or plants in the area?* Look for help at the Nature Conservancy or your state Natural Heritage Commission.
- *What are the animals in the area?* Look for help through your state Game and Fish Commission, Audubon Society, or Sierra Club.
- *What are the challenges facing your watershed?* Help find answers through your State Health Department or local water utility company.
- *What are the major pollution concerns for the area around our church?* Help find answers through the EPA's Environmental Justice Map screening tool at: https://www.epa.gov/ejscreen

Closing Prayer   (5 minutes)

Lord Jesus, we thank you that you came among us to dwell in human form, to eat the food of the earth, and live in relationship with all creation. Help us to embrace all of the bodily aspects of our lives as realities you have made holy.

Participants may add their own thanksgivings and prayers for the bodily realities of our lives: health, food, housing, clothing, and the creatures and landscapes upon which we depend.

We also give you thanks for your body and blood that nourish us in the feast of the Eucharist. We thank you that in the holy food and drink of your table you have reminded us of all the gifts of your creation.

Participants may add their own thanksgivings for the gifts of creation.

We pray now that we may endure as your body in the world. Show us how to live into the holy relationships that will lead to the health of your Church and the world that you are reconciling unto yourself.

Participants are invited to offer their prayers for the Church, all relationships, and for the reconciliation of the world.

Ecology, Part 2

Objectives

- To understand the basic elements of the ecosystems to which we are connected and the challenges that may face them
- To learn how to map our connections to different important factors, like our watershed, and focus deeply on one factor at a time
- To understand how our life as the Church has a role in the care of our particular ecosystems

Materials

- ❏ Flip chart
- ❏ Markers
- ❏ Pens
- ❏ Paper
- ❏ Post-it Notes®

- ❏ Chart paper with "3 Key Factors of Church" written on it: 1. Truth-Telling Community; 2. Agent of God's Work; 3. Vision of Hope for the Future
- ❏ Chart paper with "Ecclesia → Ecology" (written in bold print)
- ❏ Church Property Map
- ❏ Geographic Map
- ❏ Local maps of the city or county that include its geology and hydrology. These are available from your state geological survey or can be found using Google Earth.
- ❏ One copy of *Church, Creation, and the Common Good* for each participant who did not receive one in a previous session

Reminders for the Facilitator

- Organize and set up the room and materials ahead of time.
- Pray for all the participants before each session.
- Keep the conversation flowing, making room for all to share.
- Be open to listening more than sharing.
- Let the process unfold organically for each participant.

Welcome and Opening Prayer   (5 minutes)

Welcome the group back to the class. Give everyone time to find a seat. If there is anyone who is new to the class, let them introduce themselves.

During the last class we started to connect Ecclesia (the Church) to Ecology (our home), the place where we live. In this session, we will continue to look more deeply at our Ecology and focus on specific parts of it in relation to the connections and challenges that we see.

Begin with an opening prayer. Read aloud the following prayer or ask for a volunteer to share it with the class.

Many and great, O God, are thy works, maker of earth
and sky.
Thy hands have set the heavens with stars; thy fingers
spread the mountains and plains.
Lo, at thy word the waters were formed; deep seas obey
thy voice.

Grant unto us communion with thee, thou star-abiding
one;
Come unto us and dwell with us: with thee are found the
gifts of life.
Bless us with life that has no end, eternal life with thee.[5]

Optional Activity: This would be a great session to invite in a
guest speaker if you are able, seek out a local expert in the environmental field who could help your church understand the connections
with your local ecosystems. Or schedule a separate meet-up time for
this to tie in with the sessions. Resources for this are in Appendix E.

Session Overview   (15 minutes)

Remind participants that, during our last class, we looked at scriptures about the body of Christ and learned that the Church is Christ's
body in our particular places.

Remind them that we started to think about the neighborhood,
the place, and the ecosystem where we live. We started to think about
what we are connected to.

Share:

Take the opportunity to invite participants to share anything
about their ecosystem that they researched and discovered. Did
anyone focus on the major trees, animals, or plants in the area? Did

---

5. "Many and Great" by Joseph Renville (translated by R. Phillip Frazier), *Dakota
Hymn*, The Hymnal 1982, #385.

anyone focus on the specific challenges facing your watershed? Or any major pollutants near your church?

Thank the group for sharing and explain that today we are going to explore our place more deeply. To help us do that, we will start by reading a reflection by the writer and farmer Wendell Berry. He offers an assortment of questions that will help us come to understand our place. Read the following excerpt or have participants take turns reading aloud portions of it:

> What has happened here? By "here" I mean wherever you live and work. What should have happened here? What is here now? What is left of the original natural endowment? What has been lost? What has been added? What is the nature, or genius, of this place? What will nature permit us to do here without permanent damage or loss? What will nature help us to do here? What can we do to mend the damages we have done? What are the limits: Of the nature of this place? Of our intelligence and ability?[6]

Questions to Ponder:

There are lots of questions and thoughts to ponder here. Spend some time in silence reflecting on the questions in this reading. Write down thoughts or ideas.

---

6. From a commencement address delivered at Northern Kentucky University, quoted in "Wendell Berry's commencement speeches" by Claire Kelley, May 15, 2014, https://www.mhpbooks.com/wendell-berrys-commencement-speeches/ (accessed March 14, 2018).

Focus for the Day

Ecology is a discipline that explores the relationships in a particular place. There are many ways to organize and think about ecological relationships, just as there are many ways to think about our human relationships, ranging from work relationships to friendships to families. All of these relationships have different ways of occupying space together.

Water is one of the fundamental linking relationships to all ecological systems, and watersheds are the geographies of these relationships. There are many different levels of watersheds, from super watersheds like the Mississippi River Watershed (which includes all of the streams and rivers that eventually flow into the Mississippi) to local watersheds that cover only a part of a city or county.

For the map relationships below, think about how each particular map fits within this watershed system. Think of your local watershed as your basic basin of relationship, your ecological "parish," and the larger watershed structures as your broader ecclesial and ecumenical connections.

(*Note:* The "My Waters" mapping tool from the EPA is helpful for finding your local watershed with a little time. The tutorial is recommended: https://epa.maps.arcgis.com/apps/webappviewer/index.html?id=ada349b90c26496ea52aab66a092593b)

Group Reflection   (20 minutes)

Split the group into three smaller groups or pairs. Give each group a relevant watershed map and a map to go with the series of questions listed below. *Optional:* Make sure each group has a large enough map to share or plenty of smaller maps for each person.

Group 1

Church Property Map

The task with this map is to look at some of the risks as well as some of the resources that have been identified on the church's property.

When outlining the possible resources, look for positive, hopeful aspects of the property:

- Do we have a stand of trees that help clean the air?
- Do we have areas that could be converted from grass lawns to spaces for native plants?
- Where does the water flow from our property?
- Where does water flow toward our property?

When outlining the possible risks, look for negative, destructive aspects of the property:

- What is the average number of miles people drive to church on Sunday?
- What kind of equipment and chemicals are used to maintain church properties?

Group 2

World Ecological Map

The task with this map is to look at how the church is connected to the larger ecological community.

When exploring the world map, ask questions, such as:

- What are the resources that we draw into our church and where do they come from?
- Where is our electricity generated?
- Where does our potable water come from?

- Where does the food we serve originate?
- Where and how is our coffee grown?

Group 3

A Local Map

When exploring this map, ask some of the following questions:

- Through roads that connect and roads that divide, who are we in relationship with on this map?
- Who are we connected with in our local political wards?
- What are some challenges these communities face?
- How do people and structures in this space affect the ecosystem?

After all groups have had plenty of time to discuss and think through their maps together, bring everyone back together. Have each group share their maps and findings with the group.

Encourage them to think about ways these maps overlap and how they differ. When thinking of our ecosystems and connections:

- What are key challenges that we face as we study all of these maps?
- What are some key hopes and possibilities we see with all of these maps?

Key Points and Next Steps   (10 minutes)

As we think of all the places and people that we are connected to and how our lives are interwoven and affect one another, we may feel overwhelmed and see only despair. On the other hand, by reflecting on these connections we may see signs of hope and opportunity to nurture healing. As we move forward in our time together, we are going to approach the latter choice. We are going to be bold and hopeful together as the Church, seeking to connect Ecclesia and Ecology in beautiful ways together. May we be evidence in our communities that something different can flourish.

In preparation for the next session:

- Spend time being prayerfully aware of all the connections you are part of.
- As you come in contact with elements of nature, stop and pray.
- As you come in contact with different groups of people, stop and pray.
- As you read or hear the news, pray over the connections that you see.

And a reminder for groups that are able to have a dedicated space or flip chart for the duration of the class: capture key ideas, words, and insights from the "ecology" section of the course. This will be helpful as we review and finish the course as well as spark interest and inform members of the congregation who are not participating in the course.

Closing Prayer   (5 minutes)

For the closing prayer, have each group look at their particular maps. Look at all the different spots on the map where there is a connection to someone or some part of creation. Let them choose their spots and prayer aloud as they feel called. This is a kind of "Prayers of the People *and* Places."

Some ideas to suggest to the group:

- Someone could pray for the power plant that generates the church's electricity, those who live near it, and the workers who are employed there as well as the landscapes mined for the coal, natural gas, or nuclear materials that fuel it.

- Someone else could pray for the lawn crew that maintains the church, for their health and safety, for the health of their families.
- Folks could pray for particular aspects of wildlife that make their home around the church, how the church could work toward their flourishing, and not do them harm.

Feel free to guide this prayer as you like. Participants can jot down words that come to mind ahead of time and take turns reading them aloud. You can simply open and close the prayer once everyone who wants to share has finished.

SESSION 5

Economy, Part 1

Objectives

- To define economy and its relationship to ecology in the context of the Church
- To begin to understand our economic relationships and take responsibility for them
- To look at some examples of churches taking responsibility for their economy in relation to the ecosystems in which they exist

Materials

- ❏ Flip chart
- ❏ Markers
- ❏ Pens
- ❏ Chart paper with "3 Key Factors of Church" written on it: 1. Truth-Telling Community; 2. Agent of God's Work; 3. Vision of Hope for the Future

❏   Chart paper with "Ecclesia → Ecology → Economy" (written in bold print)

❏   One copy of *Church, Creation, and the Common Good* for each participant who did not receive one in a previous session

Reminders for the Facilitator

- Organize and set up the room and materials ahead of time.
- Pray for all the participants before each session.
- Keep the conversation flowing, making room for all to share.
- Be open to listening more than sharing.
- Let the process unfold organically for each participant.

Welcome and Opening Prayer   (5 minutes)

Welcome the group back. Give everyone time to find a seat. If there is anyone who is new to the class, let them introduce themselves.

Review last session's explorations of Ecology by looking at maps to better understand our relationships, connections, and the challenges that we face. In this session, we are going to start looking at how we, the Church, can best care for the places where we live. Point to the poster with "Ecclesia → Ecology →" you have been using (now add *Economy* to the poster). We will reflect on what Economy means in light of all of this.

Begin with an opening prayer. Ask for a volunteer to read it aloud.

> Heavenly Father, in your Word you have given us a vision of that holy City to which the nations of the world bring their glory: Behold and visit, we pray, the cities of the earth. Renew the ties of mutual regard which form our civic life. Send us honest and able leaders. Enable us to eliminate poverty, prejudice, and oppression, that peace may prevail with righteousness, and justice with order, and

that men and women from different cultures and with differing talents may find with one another the fulfillment of their humanity; through Jesus Christ our Lord. *Amen.*[7]

Session Overview (15 minutes)

Share:

We ended the last session in prayer over the people, places, and creatures that we are connected to. You were asked to prayerfully be aware of connections throughout the week. Invite participants to briefly share any special moments that may have surfaced over the week.

Review the content of the first two sessions looking at what the Church should be; the key factors: Agents of God's Work, Truth-Telling Community, and Vision of Hope for the Future. We used the challenge of climate change to better understand how the Church should address the particular challenges of our day.

The next sessions focused on our connections to our places—*Ecology.* Through the lens of the Incarnation we were reminded of how deeply connected we are to creation.

Questions to Ponder:

When you hear the word *Economy,* what images or thoughts come to mind?

Invite the group to share some answers. Oftentimes, we think of profits, competition, and the stock market. But what if we started to look at this word in a different way?

---

7. "For Cities," *Book of Common Prayer*, 825.

Focus for the Day

Remember the root for the prefix "eco" means "home." (Refer to the chart.) Remember also that the suffix "-nomy" means the management or care of something. How can we learn to "care for" our place, our ecology, through the perspective of the Church? Again, as with the other topics we discussed, this may seem like a daunting topic to approach. Today we will be looking at some hopeful examples.

As we study and reflect on different case studies together, let us go back to the challenge of climate change. Let us think how these particular examples are approaching the issue of climate change in bold and hopeful ways.

Group Reflection   (20 minutes)

Split the class into three smaller groups or pairs. Assign each group a different case study with the series of questions to study together. Remind them that these case studies are meant to generate ideas of what we may do someday in our own church and community. Let our reflections be a time to discern what God may be calling us to do. Case studies can be found in Appendix C beginning on page 54.

Group 1

The Cornerstone Church Case Study

After reading the case study together, encourage the group to discuss the following questions:

- How is this church nurturing relationships with the people and places they are connected to?
- In what creative ways are they addressing the specific challenges of climate change in their area? How are they caring for their place?
- What are some things we can learn from the steps this church has taken?

Group 2

The Opportunity Village Case Study

After reading the case study together, encourage the group to discuss the following questions:

- How is the mission of this program nurturing the local place as well as the people living there? How are they setting an example for others?
- In what indirect, yet creative ways are they addressing the issue of climate change?
- What are things we can learn from the steps this group has taken?

Group 3

The Depaving Case Study

After reading the case study together, encourage the group to discuss the following questions:

- How is the mission of this program nurturing the local place as well as the people living there? How are they setting an example for others?
- In what indirect, yet creative ways are they addressing the issue of climate change?
- What are some things we can learn from the steps this group has taken?

Note: These are case studies that were pulled together through site visits, conversations, and research done online. Feel free to develop your own case studies that may fit better with your particular group. Depending on the season and place where you live, you may find other examples more helpful. The aim is to show examples of churches that are connected to creative action steps of hope and resilience in the face of climate change.

Key Points and Next Steps   (10 minutes)

Through these examples and through this class, we are striving to grow bolder in our steps toward taking issues like climate change seriously as a church. We are aiming to move beyond simply changing our light bulbs and recycling our bulletins. Let us seek ways together to transform our ways of living.

As we move into this next week, let us start brainstorming how our church, with our unique ecology and watershed, can begin managing our household in a way that honors God and offers hope to the world. How we can be loving examples of resilience and boldness in the face of climate change?

In preparation for the next session:

- How do we use our energy?
- How do we nurture relationships and do outreach?
- How do we manage our physical infrastructure?
- How do we use food?
- How do we use the resources required for our worship?
- Think of all the resources we use. All the desires we may have. Think also of the resources and assets we could use more creatively.

Closing Prayer   (5 minutes)

Close with a prayer for our towns and rural areas. Our households are all linked and the economies of the city and the countryside are interlinked. It is helpful for us to remember this in our prayers and in how we think about the management of each place.

> Lord Christ, when you came among us, you proclaimed the Kingdom of God in villages, towns, and lonely places: Grant that your presence and power may be known throughout this land. Have mercy upon all of us who live

and work in rural areas [especially _____]; and grant that all the people of our nation may give thanks to you for food and drink and all other bodily necessities of life, respect those who labor to produce them, and honor the land and the water from which these good things come. All this we ask in your holy Name. *Amen.*[8]

---

8. "For Towns and Rural Places," *Book of Common Prayer*, 825.

Economy, Part 2

Objectives

- To connect the three key factors of *Ecclesia* that we discussed during our first class with three key action steps of caring for our community
- To brainstorm how our household management and ecological well-being can be brought into harmony
- To think of creative ways to address climate change in our church, directly and indirectly

Materials

- ❑ Flip chart
- ❑ Markers
- ❑ Pens
- ❑ Chart paper with "3 Key Factors of Church" written on it: 1. Truth-Telling Community; 2. Agent of God's Work; 3. Vision of Hope for the Future
- ❑ Chart paper with "Ecclesia → Ecology → Economy"

❑ Note taking supplies (index cards, highlighters, various colored pens, etc.)

❑ Art supplies (colored pencils, magazine clippings, glue, scissors, cardboard, paints, brushes, etc.)

Reminders for the Facilitator

- Organize and set up the room and materials ahead of time. (You will need a table to lay out all the note taking and art supplies.)
- Pray for all the participants before each session.
- Keep the conversation flowing, making room for all to share.
- Be open to listening more than sharing.
- Let the process unfold organically for each participant.

Welcome and Opening Prayer   (5 minutes)

Welcome the group back. Give everyone time to find a seat. If there is anyone who is new to the class, let them introduce themselves.

Review the last session's discussion on how we, the Church, can best take care of the places we live. Reference the poster with "Ecclesia → Ecology → Economy." Today we will continue to reflect on what Economy means in light of all of this.

Begin with an opening prayer. Read aloud the following prayer or invite a volunteer share it.

> Almighty and everlasting God, increase in us the gifts of faith, hope, and charity; and, that we may obtain what you promise, make us love what you command; through Jesus Christ our Lord, who lives and reigns with you and the Holy Spirit, one God, for ever and ever. *Amen.*[9]

---

9. "Collect for Proper 25, " *Book of Common Prayer*, 235.

Session Overview   (15 minutes)

We ended the last session thinking about the different resources we use and the needs/wants we have as individuals and as a church. You were asked to reflect upon ways we, as a church, could be a hopeful example to others of how to live boldly in a time of climate crisis. How could we "manage our household" in right ways?

Share:

Invite everyone to briefly share any ideas that may have surfaced over the week.

Focus for the Day

Review where we have been and where we are going:

- *Ecclesia*—Seeing the Church as a Truth-Telling Community, as an Agent of God's Work, and as a Vision of Hope for the Future
- *Ecology*—Ways in which the Church is called to be Christ's incarnation in our place; understanding our connections
- *Economy*—Exploring how our church might take responsibility for management of our home places with love and hope

If you have been collecting charts for each section along the way, this is a good time to display and review them. These will be a helpful point of reference for the practical discussions that follow.

How do we move forward together in prayer and action now that we understand our church community can live fully into an economy that nurtures all of creation?

In this final class, we are going to work together to create an action plan. Let us open our hearts to one another and to where God is leading us as we explore this path together.

Group Reflection   (25 minutes)

Share the following verse with the class:

> And now these three remain: faith, hope and love. But the
> greatest of these is love.—1 Corinthians 13:13 (NIV)

Faith, hope, and love have long been the foundations of the
Christian life.

- How can we understand our economy as a church when
  thinking of faith, hope, and love?
- How can we live into this time of climate crisis, keeping
  these key factors of the Church in mind? Let us explore this
  together in groups.

Break into three smaller groups or pairs. Give each group a different part of the verse and series of questions to study together. Remind
them that these verses and questions are meant to generate ideas for
specific projects we could pursue in our own church and community.
Encourage them to discern what God may be calling us to do.

Each group should come up with an action plan for a project
that the church could pursue. Encourage them to allow their creative
juices to flow to develop works of art, skits, charts, etc., to be pre-
sented to the whole group.

Note: Some groups may want this portion of the class to take
place over a few weeks. This does not have to be a one-time event.
The main point of this session is to spark ideas that will hopefully
lead to actions that will hopefully lead to habits for the church.

As they brainstorm action plans for their church to pursue,
remind them to think about hopeful examples they may have seen
before—from the case studies or elsewhere. Remind them to think
from a positive perspective of what the church is doing well and could
grow deeper in. Encourage them to think creatively and to be bold
with their ideas. Don't be afraid to come up with a wild plan!

Group 1

The focal point of "Faith" within 1 Corinthians 13:13

Faith is about trust, in God and one another. We depend on the gifts of creation and the labor of others. Faith is also about integrity. To be faithful is to have integrity. Some questions to ponder:

- When you think of "faith," what key words come to mind?
- How might we be faithful, with integrity, in our church's use of these resources?
- How would we relate to water, food, waste, and land?

Come up with an action plan based on your discussion. How might you offer the group and your church a faithful example of living into a right economy? Think beyond using energy-efficient light bulbs and recycling. Dig deeper into thinking of a new way of being the Church.

Group 2

The focal point of "Hope" within 1 Corinthians 13:13

Hope is living in the expectation of the world God is bringing about. Hope is what drives our life as a Vision for the Future. Some questions to ponder:

- When you think of "hope," what key words comes to mind?
- If we are to be a hopeful community, with our focus on the flourishing life God is bringing into the world, what does that look like?
- How does that affect our economy, and our care for our place?

Think about how our particular church might embody hope in this particular community as a witness to the flourishing life God wants to usher into the world. Come up with an action plan based on your discussion.

Group 3

The focal point of "Love" within 1 Corinthians 13:13

God is love. This is a self-giving kind of love devoted to the care of others. This is a love that is overflowing and never-ending. Some questions to ponder:

- When you think of "love," what key words come to mind?
- If we think of living into this agape kind of love, how might our church address the climate crisis of our generation and future generations to come?
- How might we use our household resources, our economy, to offer love to our neighbors?
- How might our church offer love to our community, including both the people and wildlife we are connected to?

Come up with an action plan based on their discussion. Give groups plenty of time to prepare their projects. If possible, let them get started with the intention of meeting again to continue their work. This will all depend on your particular group's needs and limitations.

Bring groups back together to share their ideas. Let each group share their project idea one at a time. Encourage other groups to take notes. This is an opportunity for everyone to learn from one another and to come up with a plan for moving forward on these ideas together.

Next Steps   (5 minutes)

Distribute blank index cards to everyone. Have each person write down one action step they are going to commit to based on the presentations given today. Ask them not to include recycling, solar panels, or energy efficiency. They are important, but we need to think beyond them. Encourage them to keep in mind all that they've focused on these last weeks. What has continued to surface for them?

Now have the group flip over their cards. If there is time, ask the group for one action step they will commit to take as a group. Discuss and come up with an idea. It is okay to commit to more than one idea. Write this (or these) down on the card.

Let these cards be a reminder to pray for God's guidance of how to be a church that cares for the needs of our home place. A church community that offers hope in this time of climate change—together, one step at a time.

Closing Prayer   (5 minutes)

Remind the group of the earlier classes when we used different versions of "Prayers of the People." (See Appendix B and the closing prayers from Session 3 [page 22] and 4 page 31).

The basic format for the Prayers of the People according to the *Book of Common Prayer* is as follows:

> "Prayer is offered with intercession for
> The Universal Church, its members, and its mission
> The Nation and all in authority
> The welfare of the world
> The concerns of the local community
> Those who suffer and those in any trouble
> The departed (with commemoration of a saint when
>   appropriate)"[10]

As a closing prayer for this program, have a participant lead the "popcorn" prayers of the people, covering each area, but changed according to our study (see Appendix B on page 51 as a suggested format). Specifically lift up the actions steps written on the cards in the preceding section under the "Universal Church." Include both intersessions and praises. For the requests, the response could be "Lord, hear our prayer." For the praises, the response could be "Glory, Hallelujah!" The facilitator can create the format that is appropriate for the group's context.

---

10. *Book of Common Prayer*, 383.

APPENDIX A

Scripture and Prayer

Group 1

The following prayer is prayed as a part of the dedication and consecration of a church. What does it tell us about what a church is?

> Almighty God, we thank you for making us in your image, to share in the ordering of your world. Receive the work of our hands in this place, now to be set apart for your worship, the building up of the living, and the remembrance of the dead, to the praise and glory of your Name; through Jesus Christ our Lord. *Amen.*[11]

What does it mean for us to "share in the ordering of [God's] world"?

---

11. *Book of Common Prayer*, 567.

The prayer indicates that part of the role of the church is for the worship of God, building up of the living, remembrance of the dead, and to praise and glorify God's name. How are these things accomplished in our church?

Group 2

Read the following passage from Romans. It looks at both the Church and the whole creation as they move into God's plan of salvation.

> I consider that the sufferings of this present time are not worth comparing with the glory about to be revealed to us. For the creation waits with eager longing for the revealing of the children of God; for the creation was subjected to futility, not of its own will but by the will of the one who subjected it, in hope that the creation itself will be set free from its bondage to decay and will obtain the freedom of the glory of the children of God. We know that the whole creation has been groaning in labor pains until now; and not only the creation, but we ourselves, who have the first fruits of the Spirit, groan inwardly while we wait for adoption, the redemption of our bodies. For in hope we were saved. Now hope that is seen is not hope. For who hopes for what is seen? But if we hope for what we do not see, we wait for it with patience.—Romans 8:18–25

What does this passage say about the Church and its relationship with the whole of the creation?

What does this passage say about our relationship with the present world? Does this passage say that the present world is disappearing or does it say it is being transformed?

Now read the following passage from Paul's letter to the Galatians:

> So let us not grow weary in doing what is right, for we will reap at harvest time, if we do not give up. So then, whenever we have an opportunity, let us work for the good of all, and especially for those of the family of faith.—Galatians 6:9–10

What does it tell us about the Church and how the Church should relate to the world?

Why is persistence an important part of being the Church? What does it have to do with faithfulness?

What does Paul's call to "work for the good of all, and especially for those of the family of faith" mean?

Group 3

What does this prayer for the Church tell us about what it means to be the Church?

Gracious Father, we pray for thy holy Catholic Church. Fill it with all truth, in all truth with all peace. Where it is corrupt, purify it; where it is in error, direct it; where in any thing it is amiss, reform it. Where it is right, strengthen it; where it is in want, provide for it; where it is divided, reunite it; for the sake of Jesus Christ thy Son our Savior. Amen.[12]

The first petition of the prayer is for the Church to be filled with "all truth." Why is it important that the Church be filled with "all truth"?

The petition continues by connecting "all truth with all peace." What is the connection between Truth and peace?

What would it look like for our congregation to live into "all truth with all peace"? How do we see God doing this among us now?

---

12. "Collect For the Church," *Book of Common Prayer*, 816.

APPENDIX B

Prayers of the People

Prayers of the People, Form I[13]

With all our heart and with all our mind, let us pray to the Lord, saying:

Lord, have mercy.

For the peace from above, for the loving-kindness of God, and for the salvation of our souls, let us pray to the Lord.

Lord, have mercy.

For the peace of the world, for the welfare of the Holy Church of God, and for the unity of all peoples, let us pray to the Lord.

Lord, have mercy.

For our Bishop, and for all the clergy and people, let us pray to the Lord.

Lord, have mercy.

For our president, for the leaders of all nations, and for all in authority, let us pray to the Lord.

Lord, have mercy.

---

13. *Book of Common Prayer*, 383–385.

For this city (town, village), for every city and community, and for those who live in them, let us pray to the Lord.
Lord, have mercy.

For seasonable weather, and for an abundance of the fruits of the earth, let us pray to the Lord.
Lord, have mercy.

For the good earth, which God has given us, and for the wisdom and will to conserve it, let us pray to the Lord.
Lord, have mercy.

For those who travel on land, on water, or in the air [or through outer space], let us pray to the Lord.
Lord, have mercy.

For the aged and infirm, for the widowed and orphans, and the sick and the suffering, let us pray to the Lord.
Lord, have mercy.

For the poor and the oppressed, for the unemployed and the destitute, for prisoners and captives, and for all who remember and care for them, let us pray to the Lord.
Lord, have mercy.

For all who have died in the hope of the resurrection, and for all the departed, let us pray to the Lord.
Lord, have mercy.

For deliverance from all danger, violence, oppression, and degradation, let us pray to the Lord.
Lord, have mercy.

For the absolution and remission of our sins and offenses, let us pray to the Lord.
Lord, have mercy.

That we may end our lives in faith and hope, without suffering and without reproach, let us pray to the Lord.
Lord, have mercy.

Defend us, deliver us, and in thy compassion protect us, O Lord, by thy grace.
Lord, have mercy.

In the communion of [and of all the] saints, let us commend ourselves, and one another, and all our life, to Christ our God.
To thee, O Lord our God.

Example "Popcorn" Prayers of the People

For the Church, that it may tell the Truth, live into hope, and inhabit the world faithfully.
Intersessions and praises

For our watersheds, our ecosystems and bioregions, and all of the people and powers that affect them.
Intersessions and praises

For the earth you have made, that your peace and hope will fill it.
Intersessions and praises

For our local watershed, and the cities and towns and households within it.
Intersessions and praises

For all those who suffer and whose flourishing is impeded.
Intersessions

For those who have died and for those whose witness and legacy guide us.
Intersessions and praises

APPENDIX C

Case Studies

Case Study 1: Cornerstone Church

Cornerstone United Methodist Church is located on the Eastern edge of Naples, Florida. This is a community that is directly threatened by some of the worst effects of climate change, including stronger and more frequent hurricanes and significant sea level rise. *Note:* Find Naples, Florida on a map. Take note of the area and what surrounds it.

Cornerstone has responded to these large-scale challenges of climate change in creative ways. They strive to deepen their understanding of the local ecosystems they are part of. They have found ways to live more sustainably within their ecosystems and have created models for others to learn from.

When Pastor Roy Terry realized that his church had no idea which watershed they lived in, he asked his congregation to look and find out. They discovered that they are in the Corkscrew Swamp Watershed, an ecologically significant watershed with an Audubon Society preserve at its center. The church responded by beginning to lead regular field trips to the preserve and understand their local ecosystem.

On the church's property they began an organic permaculture garden that includes perennials such as fruit trees as well as annuals. It provides food supply to neighbors and members of the church alike. The garden has become an important gathering place for conversation in the community and has resulted in significant changes. One member who managed pesticide applications for large-scale tomato growers in the area was skeptical that an organic garden could work in insect-abundant Florida. When he saw that it was possible, he then changed his mind and has reduced the amount of pesticides used on the acres he manages.

Cornerstone also serves as a staging ground for disaster relief after major weather events in the area such as hurricanes and tornadoes. They actively help their neighbors when the worst of climate change happens in their community.

Feel free to add more to this case study. For more information go to the church's website at http://www.cornerstonenaples.org/

Case Study 2: Church of the Resurrection

The Reverend Brent Was, the rector of Church of the Resurrection in Eugene, Oregon, sometimes likes to play the role of apocalyptic preacher. "The end is near," he said to a gathering of Episcopal theologians and resource managers as he described the changes to our climate that will alter the patterns of life on the planet. In the face of these challenges, however, Was has hope in the church's ability to become a community of resilience in the face of such threats.

Inspired by the Catholic Worker, Peter Maurin, he said that every house should have a Christ room and every parish should have a house of hospitality ready to receive "ambassadors of God."[14] Was and his

---

14. http://www.catholicworker.org/petermaurin/pm-biography.html (accessed March 13, 2018).

church began to build a temporary housing structure in their church parking lot. This work moved to three "tiny homes" that now sit in the parking lot and host three men who would otherwise be unsheltered.

These men are welcomed into the church community and are a witness to the poor who are always to be in our midst. They also have lessons to teach on how to live with less in a society of over abundance.

As ecological thinker Wendell Berry has written, "We all live by robbing nature, but our standard of living demands that the robbery shall continue. We must achieve the character and acquire the skills to live poorer than we do."[15] At this Episcopal Church the poor are not seen simply as the recipients of charity but as those who have the skills we all need to learn.

The tiny houses in the church parking lot have also been a public witness to the community. Was says that the church is beginning to be known as "the church with the tiny houses." This is an important public witness to the different kind of life churches can cultivate in the world.

Feel free to add more to this case study. For more information on the work of Church of the Resurrection visit their website at https://resurrectioneugene.org.

Case Study 3: Depaving Group

The landscapes of many churches are made up of parking lots. This is an unnatural structure that often contributes to the build-up of pollution in local streams through run-off water.

As Hurricane Harvey in 2017 demonstrated, paved surfaces also pose significant threats to cities. The best place for rainwater to go is into the ground where it falls, but parking lots and impermeable

15. Wendell Berry. "Word and Flesh" in *What Are People For?* (Berkley, CA: Counterpoint, 2010), 201.

surfaces block that natural process. With the increased torrential rains that climate change brings, addressing this problem is of critical importance.

Pilgrim Lutheran Church in Portland, Oregon took a step in the right direction as it worked with a local urban ecology group called *Depave*. This is a group that strips away portions of parking lots and transforms them into "rain gardens." The process allows rain to soak into the ground rather than run off into streams.

Pilgrim Church's decision to "depave" brought together church and community members in a shared space for all to use.

The values of Depave offer a vision for the economic engagement of urban churches. As Depave describes its work on its website:

> Depave empowers community members to change their surroundings from pavement to thriving landscapes that bring people together, foster stewardship, increase safety, augment play and learning spaces, provide places to grow food, capture storm water, and add to the urban tree canopy.

Feel free to add more to this case study. For more information go to the Depave website at http://www.depave.org.

You can also create an example from a recent story in your community for these case studies.

APPENDIX D

Key Facts About Climate Change

These are only a few facts from the wealth of information available about climate change. Each website cited here is worth exploring for much more information.

"The planet's average surface temperature has risen about 2.0 degrees Fahrenheit (1.1 degrees Celsius) since the late 19th century, a change driven largely by increased carbon dioxide and other human-made emissions into the atmosphere. Most of the warming occurred in the past 35 years, with 16 of the 17 warmest years on record occurring since 2001."—NASA[16]

"Human activities have affected the land, oceans, and atmosphere, and these changes have altered global climate patterns. Burning fossil fuels, releasing chemicals into the atmosphere, reducing the amount of forest cover, and rapid expansion of farming, development, and

---

16. https://climate.nasa.gov/evidence/

industrial activities are releasing carbon dioxide into the atmosphere and changing the balance of the climate system."—climate.gov[17]

"Over the coming 25 or 30 years, scientists say, the climate is likely to gradually warm, with more extreme weather. Coral reefs and other sensitive habitats are already starting to die. Longer term, if emissions rise unchecked, scientists fear climate effects so severe that they might destabilize governments, produce waves of refugees, precipitate the sixth mass extinction of plants and animals in the Earth's history, and melt the polar ice caps, causing the seas to rise high enough to flood most of the world's coastal cities. The emissions that create those risks are happening now, raising deep moral questions for our generation."—*The New York Times*[18]

"Climatic conditions affect diseases transmitted through water, and via vectors such as mosquitoes. Climate-sensitive diseases are among the largest global killers. Diarrhea, malaria, and protein-energy malnutrition alone caused more than 3 million deaths globally in 2004, with over one third of these deaths occurring in Africa."—World Health Organization[19]

"The majority of modeling studies agree that climate change impacts on crop yields will be negative from the 2030s onwards. Nearly half of projections beyond 2050 indicate yield decreases greater than 10%."—Research Program on Climate Change, Agriculture, and Food Security[20]

---

17. https://www.climate.gov/teaching/essential-principles-climate-literacy/essential-principles-climate-literacy
18. https://www.nytimes.com/interactive/2017/climate/what-is-climate-change.html
19. http://www.who.int/features/factfiles/climate_change/facts/en/index7.html
20. https://ccafs.cgiar.org/bigfacts/#theme=climate-impacts-production

APPENDIX E

Climate Change Resources

There is so much information available about climate change. Below are just a few suggestions to help get you started. Some groups may decide to read a book or watch a full movie and have a discussion. We highly recommend both the book and video titled *This Changes Everything* noted below.

Books

Naomi Klein. *This Changes Everything: Capitalism vs. the Climate* (New York: Simon & Schuster, 2014).

> Written by the activist Naomi Klein, this book explores our dire climate situation and the underlying causes rooted in industrial capitalism. While pessimistic about the solutions, Klein offers a hopeful call for a movement rooted in placed communities around the world who love their landscapes and waters.

Bill McKibben. *Earth: Making a Life on a Tough New Planet* (New York: St. Martin's Griffin, 2011).

> Bill McKibben's *The End of Nature* was the first popular book about climate change. This more recent book outlines the drastic changes happening to our planet and offers some hopeful paths toward a solution, if we act soon.

Elizabeth Koblert. *The Sixth Extinction: An Unnatural History* (New York: Henry Holt, 2014).

> This Pulitzer Prize-winning book explores how human activity is doing what asteroids and ice ages accomplished in the past: mass extinction. Kolbert is a wonderful storyteller with an ability to make science lively for the average reader and yet pulls no punches as to the reality human beings are creating.

Dale Jamieson. *Reason in a Dark Time: Why the Struggle Against Climate Change Failed—and What It Means for Our Future* (New York: Oxford UP, 2014).

> Jamieson is a philosopher who was active in early climate negotiations. While he believes we can still act to blunt some of the worst effects of climate change, he recognizes that our chance for significant action has passed and we are now stuck with significant warming. What that means for how we now live is the theme of his provocative and important book.

Jeff Goodell. *The Water Will Come: Rising Seas, Sinking Cities, and the Remaking of the Civilized World* (New York: Little Brown, 2017).

> This new book examines how sea level rise is coming and what it will mean for our civilization, from sinking coasts to international refugee crises.

Videos

This Changes Everything
https://thischangeseverything.org/

> This video companion to the book by the same title offers
> an important look at the underlying narratives that created
> the climate crisis and the efforts by people working at the
> grass roots level all around the world to change our way of
> life, so that we can live in balance with the earth.

Merchants of Doubt
http://www.merchantsofdoubt.org/

> Climate change denial is not the result of difficult facts,
> but due to a concerted effort by vested interests to sow
> doubt. This documentary looks at those interests and their
> agents and shows how powerful lobbies have hindered our
> efforts to combat climate change.

Years of Living Dangerously
http://yearsoflivingdangerously.com/

> This is a series from Showtime that explores both the sci-
> ence of climate change and the stories that intersect with
> it. Episode 4 of Season 1, "Ice & Brimstone," is particu-
> larly helpful for church audiences since it follows a young
> Christian woman's effort to convince her pastor-father of
> the reality of climate change.

Global Weirding with Katherine Hayhoe
https://www.youtube.com/channel/UCi6RkdaEqgRVKi3AzidF4ow
/videos

> Katherine Hayhoe is a Christian climate scientist who
> is excellent at communicating climate science clearly,

especially for those on the skeptical side. This YouTube channel is a series sponsored by PBS. There is a lot to explore here, but all worth a look.

National and International Websites

United States Geological Survey Climate Change Viewer
https://www2.usgs.gov/climate_landuse/clu_rd/nccv.asp

> This tool from the USGS allows you to explore how climate change will potentially affect local temperatures, rainfall, and soil.

Catholic Climate Movement
https://catholicclimatemovement.global/

> This website offers a host of resources, prayers, and ideas for action from the Roman Catholic Church, most of which are useful for Christians of all denominations. Their "stories of climate impacts" do a wonderful job of making the abstract realities of climate change visible in the affects they are having on people's lives.

The Environmental Protection Agency's (EPA) Environmental Justice Map screening tool: https://www.epa.gov/ejscreen

> This tool from the EPA allows you to explore various pollutants and toxins in your city and neighborhood.

What Could Disappear
http://www.nytimes.com/interactive/2012/11/24/opinion/sunday/what-could-disappear.html

> This website from *The New York Times* explores various sea level rise scenarios and how they will affect several major U.S. cities.

Your State or Local Websites:

The resources and titles of agencies vary from state to state, but these types of entities typically have useful resources for learning your watershed.

- Natural Heritage Commission
- Game and Fish Commission
- Local Water Utility
- State Health Department
- Organizations such as the Sierra Club (sierraclub.org), Nature Conservancy (nature.org), and Audubon Society (audubon. org) all have local organizations that should have a wealth of resources about your local ecosystems and the effects of climate change. These are also good places to check for guest speakers as many of these organizations have professional scientists on staff.